LOS ANGELES

THE CITY AT A GLANCE

C000212336

Echo Park
Check out the increasingly fa[mous]
cafés and shops around Alva[rado]
and W Sunset Boulevard.

Dodger Stadium
One of America's most pleasant ballparks,
once home to the Latino community of
Chavez Ravine, which was forced out to make
way for the LA Dodgers' new home.
1000 Elysian Park Avenue, T 323 224 2966

777 Tower
This 52-storey white-steel-and-glass tower,
designed by Pelli Clarke Pelli Architects,
is just distinctive enough to stand out from
the Downtown crowd.
777 S Figueroa Street

Walt Disney Concert Hall
Buried among the skyscrapers, Frank Gehry's
home for the Los Angeles Philharmonic is an
absolute must-see, inside and out.
See p014

Little Tokyo
Order great sushi and sashimi at restaurant
and gallery R23 (see p032) and shop for pots
at Little Tokyo Clayworks (T 213 617 7193).

Caltrans District 7 Headquarters
For some, this building suggests the aliens
have landed in Downtown; for the Pritzker
jury, Thom Mayne's transport HQ represents
the rootless nature of the city.
See p010

San Gabriel Mountains
In winter, Angelenos like to retreat to the San
Gabriels for a spot of snowboarding. Summer
can see search and rescue picking up hikers
with no way down from a mountain ledge.

INTRODUCTION
THE CHANGING FACE OF THE URBAN SCENE

It's long been easy to knock LA. Even Raymond Chandler, the city's laureate, called it a 'big hard-boiled city, with no more personality than a paper cup', lambasting the 'drab anonymity of a thousand shabby lives' lived out there. And that was in the good times. Well, things have changed, and almost a decade into the 21st century, LA is holding its own as a lure for commercial and cultural heavy-hitters. Tourism shows no sign of slowing, and its media industries continue to thrive, in spite of the economic crunch.

Across the city, this new-found confidence is visible in the string of design-led bars, restaurants and hotels that now stretches in an arc from the <u>Hollywood Roosevelt Hotel</u> (see p029) to <u>The Penthouse at The Huntley Hotel</u> (see p046) in more sedate Santa Monica. Revived neighbourhoods such as Silver Lake and Venice remain hot addresses, while even further out, East Eagle Rock and Glendale, which now has its own deluxe mall, The Americana at Brand (889 Americana Way, T 887 897 2097), boasting Tiffany, <u>Katsuya</u> (see p052) and Kitson outposts, are gentrifying fast.

The city of Eames, Neutra and 'Googie' has always had few equals in its appreciation of challenging architecture and interiors, and it shows in the rows of stores still stocking Danish midcentury sideboards and the star status given to the people creating the look of today's LA. The city remains a bellwether for the kind of high-end design that, one day, will be the backdrop to all our leisure hours.

ESSENTIAL INFO
FACTS, FIGURES AND USEFUL ADDRESSES

TOURIST OFFICE
Hollywood & Highland Center
6801 Hollywood Boulevard
T 323 467 6412
discoverlosangeles.com

TRANSPORT
Car hire
Avis
T 310 342 9200
Metro (buses and trains)
T 213 922 6000
metro.net
Taxis
ITS Limo
T 310 551 3159
Yellow Cab
T 310 808 1000

EMERGENCY SERVICES
Emergencies
T 911
Police (non-emergencies)
Central Community Police Station
251 E Sixth Street
T 213 485 3294
24-hour pharmacy
CVS
2530 Glendale Boulevard
T 323 666 1285

CONSULATES
British Consulate
Suite 1200, 11766 Wilshire Boulevard
T 310 481 0031
britainusa.com

MONEY
American Express
8493 W Third Street/La Cienega Boulevard
T 310 659 1682
travel.americanexpress.com

POSTAL SERVICES
Post Office
300 N Los Angeles Street
T 800 275 8777
Shipping
UPS
3183 Wilshire Boulevard
T 213 351 1338
ups.com

BOOKS
Building The Getty by Richard Meier
(University of California Press)
**Deco Landmarks: Art Deco Gems
of Los Angeles** by Arnold Schwartzman
and Bevis Hillier (Chronicle Books)
John Lautner, Architect by Frank Escher
(Princeton Architectural Press)

WEBSITES
Architecture/Design
modaagallery.com
sciarc.edu
Art
getty.edu
lacma.org
moca.org
Newspapers
latimes.com
laweekly.com

COST OF LIVING
Taxi from LAX airport to Hollywood
£35
Cappuccino
£2.30
Packet of cigarettes
£3
Daily newspaper
£0.90
Bottle of champagne
£85

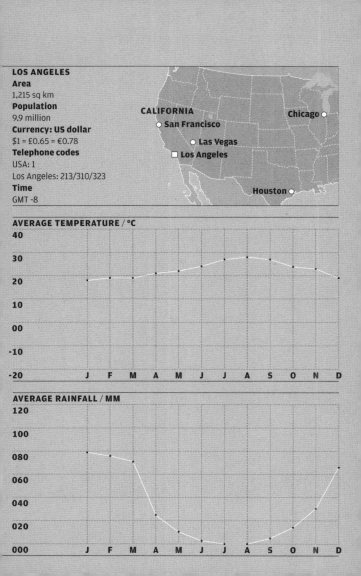

LOS ANGELES
Area
1,215 sq km
Population
9.9 million
Currency: US dollar
$1 = £0.65 = €0.78
Telephone codes
USA: 1
Los Angeles: 213/310/323
Time
GMT -8

CALIFORNIA

San Francisco

Las Vegas

Los Angeles

Chicago

Houston

AVERAGE TEMPERATURE / °C

40											
30											
20											
10											
00											
-10											
-20	J	F	M	A	M	J	J	A	S	O	N	D

AVERAGE RAINFALL / MM

120											
100											
080											
060											
040											
020											
000	J	F	M	A	M	J	J	A	S	O	N	D

NEIGHBOURHOODS

THE AREAS YOU NEED TO KNOW AND WHY

To help you navigate the city, we've chosen the most interesting districts (see below and the map inside the back cover) and colour-coded our featured venues, according to their location; those venues that are outside these areas are not coloured.

WEST HOLLYWOOD AND MIDTOWN

A contender for the heart of the western side of the city, WeHo is home to LA's gay district and, not coincidentally, some of its most sumptuous designer shopping on tiny Melrose Place. There are plenty of places to eat and be seen, in addition to an ever-growing list of hip hotels, such as The London (see p026), and, of course, the unmissable Chateau Marmont (see p020).

SANTA MONICA, VENICE AND CULVER CITY

Santa Monica has always been affluent and liberal, but a few recent openings, such as the revamped Hotel Shangri-La (see p016), have given it a new edge. Artsy Venice's Abbot Kinney Boulevard has long been rattling to the sound of the gentrifiers' hammers in a process that is very nearly complete, while Culver City's burgeoning restaurants, furniture stores and galleries have made this once-forgettable 'burb worth a visit.

HOLLYWOOD

Hollywood Boulevard is awash with tourist tat, but the area's side streets are home to hip clubs and restaurants, usually owned by movie money, and designed by the likes of Dodd Mitchell, Thomas Schoos and Philippe Starck, such as Katsuya (see p052) and S Bar (see p060). The Hollywood and Vine intersection is the epicentre, where hot venues have been opening faster than a valet can park your Bentley Continental.

LOS FELIZ AND SILVER LAKE

Silver Lake is largely residential, but with houses designed by Richard Neutra, Rudolf M Schindler and John Lautner. It has remained chain-store-free, and boasts a clutch of interesting boutiques, destination coffee shops, such as LAMILL (1636 Silver Lake Boulevard, T 323 663 4441), and, along Silver Lake Boulevard and Vermont Avenue, slick places to eat and drink.

BEVERLY HILLS AND WESTWOOD

Up until recently, this old-money 'hood lacked panache, but the arrival of chic hotels like the Thompson (see p017) and eateries such as Luckyfish (see p041) and CUT (see p049) has changed that. Beverly Hills also retains industry magic in hidden places; check out the Fountain Coffee Room at The Beverly Hills Hotel (see p032) for a skinny latte with the movie moguls. Westwood is the home of the University of California and Richard Meier's Getty Center (see p068), with its superb views.

DOWNTOWN

There was a time when there was little in the way of culture or social life to lure anyone here and, after hours, the only people you'd come across would be the homeless. Despite years of investment and claims of a renaissance, it can still feel like a ghost town. Yet the area is in transition, and is home to two dazzling buildings: the Caltrans District 7 Headquarters (see p010) and the Walt Disney Concert Hall (see p014).

LANDMARKS

THE SHAPE OF THE CITY SKYLINE

Some of the most acclaimed film treatments of LA, from *Short Cuts* and *Pulp Fiction* to *Magnolia* and *Crash*, have been narratives that capture the city using multiple, interwoven storylines. They echo the alienating sprawl of this megalopolis and reveal its potential to put the fear of God into first-time visitors. In fact, thanks to the mountains to the north, ocean to the west and its well-signposted boulevards and freeways, LA is surprisingly easy to navigate.

But you must, must have a car. The main areas to explore lie along a curve sweeping north-west from Downtown, through Hollywood to Venice. Latino East LA and the San Fernando Valley to the north have pockets of interest, but the visitor is unlikely to have enough time to seek them out. Instead head to Silver Lake for SoCal (Southern Californian) architecture, and Downtown for more contemporary pleasures, such as the Caltrans HQ (overleaf), Frank Gehry's Walt Disney Concert Hall (see p014) and MOCA (250 S Grand Avenue, T 213 626 6222). On the north-eastern tip of Hollywood is the Seventh-Day Adventist Church (1711 N Van Ness Avenue, T 323 462 0010), a true LA landmark in that it sits at the Hollywood Freeway and Hollywood Boulevard intersection and is passed by thousands of drivers each day. Its curved concrete form has been described as a 'boat of faith, riding on a sea of humanity', or more prosaically, as 'God's own gas station'. *For full addresses, see Resources.*

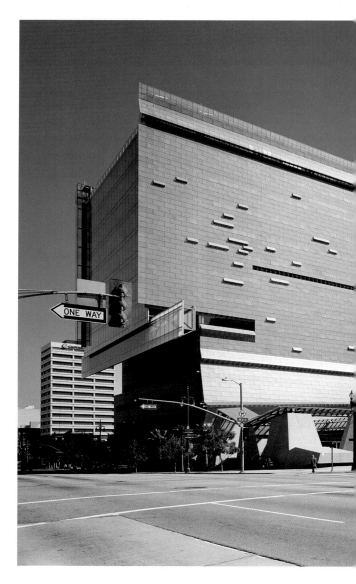

Caltrans District 7 Headquarters

This is the building that helped Thom Mayne bring the Pritzker Prize back to America in 2005, for the first time in 14 years. Likened by some detractors to the Death Star, the Caltrans HQ certainly is imposing – a matt grey steel hulk of a building that takes up a whole city block – but it is made graceful by the many perforations in its metal skin, the folds and openings of which break up the structure's lines. Keith Sonnier's neon installation, *Motordom*, attached to the building itself and suggestive of brake lights on an LA freeway, adds some much-needed levity. If you stand on the north-west corner of the junction of Broadway and First Street, you can see the Walt Disney Concert Hall (see p014) and Caltrans HQ at the same time.
100 S Main Street

Norms Restaurant

Everyone has their favourite 'Googie', a nickname given to a style of modern architecture introduced by John Lautner in 1949. Pann's in Inglewood (T 310 670 1441) is often cited as the best example, but it's not exactly central. Norms is in the heart of West Hollywood and doesn't feel like a tourist attraction or an architecture museum. It's a living structure, a little shabby at the edges and in need of some new ceiling tiles, but worth a visit for its space-age lampshades alone. It's also a handy place to while away a few hours, drink endless cups of coffee and chat to some down-to-earth locals at the lunch counter, should you tire of discussing Hans Wegner chairs around the corner on Beverly Boulevard.

470 N La Cienega Boulevard,
T 323 655 0167, normsrestaurants.com

Capitol Records Building

Drive south on the 101 Freeway into Hollywood, and the first thing you'll see, through the smog, off the Vine Street exit, is Welton Becket & Associates' 1956 Capitol Records. Resembling a stack of discs, it was the world's first circular office building and is topped with a 'stylus needle' that is reputed to blink out 'Hollywood' in Morse code. Fittingly, you have to step over John Lennon's star on the Hollywood Walk of Fame to enter the gold-record-lined lobby. Capitol still has a working in-house recording studio, where orchestras lay down tracks for the big awards shows. Knowing that The Beatles, Beach Boys and Frank Sinatra have all walked through its doors makes this a landmark many times over.

1750 Vine Street, T 323 462 6252, capitolrecords.com

Walt Disney Concert Hall
It has been described as a barge at full sail, a homage to the billowing skirts of Marilyn Monroe, a cubist masterpiece, and a physical manifestation of a certain cartoon mouse's strokes with his magic wand. It is, in fact, stunningly beautiful, universally lauded and a home-town stainless-steel victory for its designer, Frank Gehry. Some say it surpasses his Guggenheim Museum in Bilbao. Years of funding problems and delays almost killed the project, but following its opening in 2003, Gehry's building became the big, shiny hope of the city fathers, who prayed that it would bring some life back to the moribund Downtown zone. If you get a chance, go to a concert (it's the home of the Los Angeles Philharmonic), if only to see the undulating form of the interior.
111 S Grand Avenue, T 323 850 2000, laphil.com

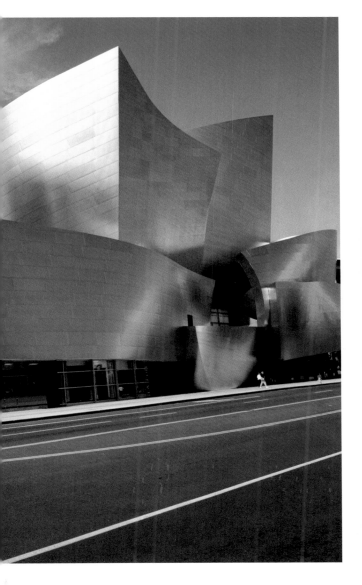

HOTELS

WHERE TO STAY AND WHICH ROOMS TO BOOK

LA has always been famous for its hotels, but the plethora of chic berths opened in recent years has given the city a reputation for strong contemporary design for the first time in decades. The people to thank for this include André Balazs, whose midcentury-meets-Gothic revamp kept Chateau Marmont (see p020) on top of the pile in the early 1990s. Moving across Sunset Boulevard, he then created the once ice-cool, now lukewarm The Standard Hollywood (8300 Sunset Boulevard, T 323 650 9090), following this with The Standard Downtown (see p024). Then came his chief rivals Brad Korzen and Kelly Wearstler, who took the Beverly Carlton Hotel and furnished it to create a modernist haven, the Avalon (see p028). Next they opened the tiny Maison 140 (140 S Lasky Drive, T 310 281 4000) and then the Viceroy (see p030).

The latest wave is a mix of revamps and brand-new hotels. Among the renovations are Benjamin Noriega-Ortiz's reworking of the Mondrian (8440 Sunset Boulevard, T 323 650 8999), and a multimillion-dollar overhaul of Santa Monica's landmark art deco Hotel Shangri-La (1301 Ocean Avenue, T 310 394 2791). Meanwhile, the SBE group collaborated with Philippe Starck on the hotly anticipated SLS (465 N La Cienega Boulevard, T 310 247 0400), Avi Brosh opened Palihouse (overleaf) and David Collins designed the interiors for LA's answer to NYC's The London (see p026). *For full addresses and room rates, see Resources.*

Thompson Beverly Hills

Thompson Hotels has transplanted some much-needed sophistication from the Big Apple into the previously forgettable Beverly Pavilion. Architect and designer Dodd Mitchell, a key player in Hollywood's renaissance, has worked his magic once again, merging urban modernism with the laid-back but elegant SoCal style. All 107 rooms, such as the King Superior (above), are inspired by the yin and yang of 1960s Hollywood glamour and boho New York cool; in particular the Penthouse Suite with its white walls, dark dressers and oak floor. Jonathan Morr's BondSt (T 310 601 2255) restaurant is gaining a reputation for its superior sushi. Head up to the top-floor ABH bar, which boasts fire pits, a pool, cabanas and sweeping views. *9360 Wilshire Boulevard, T 310 273 1400, thompsonbeverlyhills.com*

Palihouse

American developer Avi Brosh's collection of long-stay 'urban lodges' opened in the heart of West Hollywood in January 2008. Each requires a minimum seven-night stay, but given the 'home-from-home' vibe here that shouldn't pose a problem. Brosh designed the entire space, which includes 36 studios and one- or two-bedroom residences. All have a loft-style feel, with many featuring brick walls, leather sofas, marble-counter kitchens, such as in Room 311 (above), and washer-dryers. We're also fans of the Holloway Loft Residence (right), which has two en suite bedrooms and private verandahs. The in-house Hall restaurant is a cosy-cool brasserie with a lovely courtyard, where you can order European fare or sip a cocktail. Should you need them, a personal trainer, shopper, translator or dog walker can be arranged.
8465 Holloway Drive, T 323 656 4100, palihouse.com

Chateau Marmont

This eccentric 1920s folly, perched above Sunset Boulevard, is still our top choice for digs in LA. The appeal of André Balazs' restored chateau is not the fact that John Belushi's life ended here, but its private bungalows, gorgeous pool and gardens, overlooked by Gothic-arched colonnades (left). And if you tire of these delights, you can settle into the lounge, where things are low-key and celeb-packed but convivial, compared to the crowded Bar Marmont. Of course, there are hotels with better rooms and bigger pools, and some place somewhere will be generating more buzz. But this is Chateau Marmont, and there isn't anywhere else quite like it.
8221 Sunset Boulevard, T 323 656 1010, chateaumarmont.com

Hotel Palomar Los Angeles-Westwood
Kimpton Hotels' Palomar, opened in April 2008, injected some much-needed cool into the Westwood area. Yes, it's a bit over the top with its high-glam interiors, but the eco-focused boutique concept is spot on. Local interior designer Cheryl Rowley has created a movie-industry haunt, inspired by stars from Marilyn Monroe to Scarlett Johansson; expect dramatic shocks of ice-blue and lipstick-red, faux-fur throws and snakeskin furniture panels in the guest rooms, such as the King Standard (above and right). Our choice is the Vista King Spa Suite, which has panoramic views and a huge bathroom with a soaking tub. The Palomar's environment-friendly draws include water- and energy-efficient devices, sustainable seafood on the menu at in-house restaurant Blvd 16, and mini-bars stocked with organic food and drinks. *10740 Wilshire Boulevard, T 310 475 8711, hotelpalomar-lawestwood.com*

The Standard Downtown
This is the place to stay Downtown (if you
have to). It's camp, but in a good way,
working it well in this macho former oil
HQ. The pluses include a fantastic all-
night retro-diner restaurant, live DJ sets
on The Rooftop Bar every night, a stunning
Vladimir Kagan-designed lobby (right),
and lots of contemporary luxe rooms,
including the Huge Room (above), which
has a tub at the bottom of the bed and
The Man from U.N.C.L.E. fixtures and
fittings. No opportunity for a double
entendre has been passed up, judging by
the pencils with 'use me' written on them
and room cards featuring the instruction
'push me in'. The risqué jokes do get
stretched pretty thin, though: the phones
include speed-dials for 'heaven', 'hell'
and a 'fluffer' – perhaps more Austin
Powers than Illya Kuryakin.
550 S Flower Street/Sixth Street,
T 213 892 8080, standardhotels.com

The London West Hollywood

One of the most heavily hyped arrivals of 2008 was LXR Luxury Resorts & Hotels' West Coast sister property to The London NYC. Set behind a busy stretch of Sunset Boulevard, the dowdy former Bel Age was transformed beyond recognition to create a hotel fusing Angeleno attitude and European sophistication. For the new suite-only venue, British interior designer David Collins chose subtle tones of teal, blue and brown, such as in the one-bedroom Suite 811 (above), while fellow Brit Gordon Ramsay launched an eponymous in-house restaurant (T 310 358 7788) – all pale pink, powder-blue and gold. The only thing that remains from the original hotel is the sprawling view from the rooftop (right). Concierge service Quintessentially is on hand to take care of all those little extra needs.
1020 N San Vicente Boulevard, T 310 854 1111, thelondonwesthollywood.com

Avalon

Kelly Wearstler's tribute to midcentury modern chic – all George Nelson lamps and Isamu Noguchi tables – opened in 1999. It soon became pretty much the hippest spot to hang out in Beverly Hills, and has managed to maintain this cachet ever since. Built from the bones of the old Beverly Carlton, once a haunt of Marilyn's, plus two adjoining apartment blocks, it was designed as an open-plan space, so that some of the guest rooms open onto balconies overlooking the pool. Pea-green walls in a few of these mute the slightly sub-*Jetsons* feel of the furnishings. The Blue on Blue restaurant/bar, with its curtained poolside cabanas (above), still draws a big crowd of beautiful folk. The vibe is fun but classy.

9400 W Olympic Boulevard, T 310 277 5221, avalonbeverlyhills.com

Hollywood Roosevelt Hotel

The tried-and-tested hotel-as-theatre strategy may have found its limits here. After its relaunch in 2005, the Roosevelt used young celebrities, parties, publicists and endless media coverage of its two nightspots, Teddy's and the Tropicana, to create a beyond-the-velvet-rope buzz. It did this so well that non-celeb guests in the hotel started to complain about exclusion. Bar manager Amanda Scheer Demme, who pulled the stars in, soon parted company with the owner Thompson Hotels (the people behind the Thompson Beverly Hills, see p017), but the Roosevelt's Dodd Mitchell-designed interiors, such as the Cabana Suites (above), and poolside Tropicana bar still make the hotel a hot destination for LA's swish set.
7000 Hollywood Boulevard,
T 323 466 7000, hollywoodroosevelt.com

Viceroy

When it opened its doors in July 2002, Kelly Wearstler declared the style of her Santa Monica hotel as 'modern with a colonial vibe', while *LA Times* design guru David A Keeps described it as new, eclectic, 21st-century Hollywood. Either way, the yellow gentlemen's-club furniture and matching 1970s-ish carpets in the library (left) and the camp mix of Regency and contemporary in the lobby (above)

work. The in-house Whist restaurant, overseen by exec chef Warren Schwartz, has a reputation for its modern American cuisine and A-list clientele. The poolside cabanas come with plasma TV screens, heaters, private waiters and an eye-popping £725 minimum spend if you want to reserve one for a chef's tasting night. *1819 Ocean Avenue, T 310 260 7500, viceroysantamonica.com*

24 HOURS
SEE THE BEST OF THE CITY IN JUST ONE DAY

The 'drive everywhere' cliché about LA is so oft-repeated that it's easy to forget you will have to walk once you get to where you're going. Downtown, Beverly Hills, Santa Monica and Venice all have strollable streets; some of them, such as Santa Monica's Third, are pedestrianised, while the Venice Canals can only be appreciated on foot. There are shops you will want to amble past, such as American Rag (150 S La Brea Avenue, T 323 935 3154) for great vintage finds, and places you'll want to go to on a whim, like R23 (923 E Second Street, T 213 687 7178), a low-key sushi joint with Frank Gehry cardboard chairs. You can also walk the trails in Griffith Park or hike the unpaved western end of Mulholland Drive. Even parts of Sunset Boulevard can be done without a car.

All the same, to do LA in a day you will have to put in some serious tarmac time. We suggest spending the morning in West Hollywood, then driving out to Malibu, to The Getty Villa (see p037), ending your day Downtown with dinner at Patina (see p038) and drinks at Blue Velvet (750 S Garland Avenue, T 213 239 0061), which has a poolside bar and great views. But being led by your satnav mustn't mean overlooking classic spots like Fred Segal (see p078) and the Fountain Coffee Room at The Beverly Hills Hotel (9641 Sunset Boulevard, T 310 276 2251), where you can indulge in a little celeb-spotting and Hollywood-golden-age nostalgia. *For full addresses, see Resources.*

09.00 BLD

A power breakfast is a key meal for the entertainment industry, and BLD offers one of the best in town. Billed as 'modern comfort food', its menu features lots of figure-conscious options, including brûléed grapefruit, while sore heads can be soothed with grilled flat-iron steak and eggs. Weekend brunch is served from 8am to 3pm, when we recommend you order chef Neal Fraser's ricotta blueberry pancake, or the Spanish scramble, with chorizo, fingerling potatoes, roasted piquillo peppers and manchego. BLD's décor adds to the sleek, stylish feel of the place – the blondwood and wheat-coloured walls given a kick by the fiery red signage and bar stools. There's also a shop, where you can stock up on gourmet snacks. *7450 Beverly Boulevard, T 323 930 9744, bldrestaurant.com*

11.00 BCAM at LACMA

The Broad Contemporary Art Museum (BCAM), and philanthropists Eli and Edythe Broad, have provided LA with a major collection of pop art. The 2008 project cost a whopping £28m but, at 5,575 sq m, LACMA now boasts, thanks to architect Renzo Piano's design, one of the largest column-free art spaces in the US. The open-air pavilion features Jeff Koons' giant sculpture *Tulips*, while inside the building, displayed amid a maze of red steel staircases, there are works by Andy Warhol, Damien Hirst, Cindy Sherman, Jean-Michel Basquiat and Roy Lichtenstein. The view from the third floor is sensational, and even the lift shaft, which is lined with Barbara Kruger's black, white and red slogan piece *Shafted*, is impressive.
5905 Wilshire Boulevard, T 323 857 6000, lacma.org

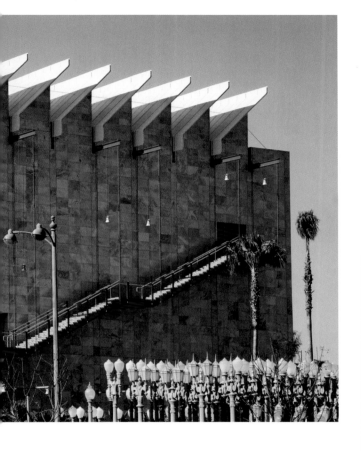

13.00 Joan's on Third

Jostle your way through the throng on the sidewalk and grab a seat at the communal table at the back, or on a sunny day sit outside. What brings so many Angelenos to this unassuming spot? Its owner Joan McNamara, assisted by daughters Carol and Susie, who feed the city's foodies with perfectly executed American classics, like macaroni cheese and turkey meatloaf. Joan's recently expanded to accommodate its growing number of fans and Southland's passion for its cupcakes. The takeaway counters now resemble giant picnic hampers, overflowing with cheeses, deli meat, breads and pastries, so whether you're eating in or out, tuck in. *8350 W Third Street, T 323 655 2285, joansonthird.com*

16.30 The Getty Villa

A rich man's folly, but oh what a folly. John Paul Getty's 1974 villa, modelled on the Roman Villa dei Papiri, buried when Vesuvius erupted in 79AD, was used to house the oil billionaire's collection of Greek, Roman and Etruscan antiquities after his death in 1976. Thirty years on, a nine-year, £150m extension of the site, by Boston-based architects Rodolfo Machado and Jorge Silvetti, helped turn The Getty Villa into one of the hottest tickets in town. Not to be confused with Richard Meier's Getty Center (see p068), the Villa's oceanside setting and acres of marble make it an irresistible spectacle in the SoCal light. This is a lovely spot to watch the sun set over a glass of wine – just make sure you book well in advance. *17985 Pacific Coast Highway, T 310 440 7300, getty.edu*

21.00 Patina
Housed in one of the aluminium 'petals'
of the Walt Disney Concert Hall (see
p014), Joachim Splichal's restaurant has
a great bar for pre-concert cocktails
and a terrace for alfresco dining. But
the main draw is Patina's top-notch
seasonal modern American cuisine. Try
the seafood or one of the tasting menus.
*141 S Grand Avenue. T 213 972 3331,
patinagroup.com*

URBAN LIFE

CAFÉS, RESTAURANTS, BARS AND NIGHTCLUBS

If you're looking to hang out, eye up the beautiful people and suck up some glamour, few places can compete with LA's Cahuenga Boulevard, Hollywood Boulevard or Sunset Strip. Traditionally, with a few noble exceptions, the city's restaurant scene was never really about the food, though that has changed recently with renowned chefs like Mario Batali (Osteria Mozza, see p058) and Todd English (Beso, see p054) heading out West. Yes, their eateries are still glam, but the food bar has been raised at long last.

Hollywood is where it's at right now. Once run-down, the area has been reinvigorated by local entertainment powerhouse SBE and movie mogul money, and hyped to the hilt thanks to the celebs who now go there. Nearby venues such as the low-key Writer's Bar at Raffles L'Ermitage (9291 Burton Way, T 310 278 3344) are now less about meeting your agent and more about being seen.

Outside Hollywood things are less precious. Santa Monica offers elegant dining venues (see p030 and p046), while the vibe is a little edgier in Venice and Silver Lake. Then, of course, there is the question of the best burger joint. Some say In-n-Out (7009 Sunset Boulevard), some say Fatburger (1611 N Vermont Avenue, T 323 663 3100), but for a real insider's junk-food tip, head to Pink's (709 N La Brea Avenue, T 323 931 4223) for a chilli dog or Roscoe's House of Chicken 'n' Waffles (1514 N Gower Street, T 323 466 7453). *For full addresses, see Resources.*

Luckyfish

The people behind this *kaiten-zushi* (conveyor-belt sushi restaurant) venue, the Innovative Dining Group, are also owners of LA favourites Sushi Roku (T 323 655 6767) and the BOA Steakhouse. (T 323 650 8383). Here, a striking wooden sculpture lures diners inside to sit at a long pebble-effect sushi counter. The design, by Tag Front, is sleek but not cold, thanks to the textured cement walls and cherry-blossom mural at the back. Electronic chips are embedded in the plates to monitor the freshness of the dishes, such as 'dragon' rolls with crab, avocado and eel; any that have rotated for more than 60 minutes are ejected. An added attraction for Angelinos is that Luckyfish purifies and bottles its own water.
338 N Canon Drive, T 310 274 9800, luckyfishsushi.com

Comme Ça

Inspired by French brasseries, chef David Myers, of Sona (T 310 659 7708) and Boule pâtisserie (see p080) fame, has scored another hit with the buzzy Comme Ça. The crisp design by LA's KAA Design Group includes long blackboards behind white tufted banquettes, antique mirrors and a picture ledge filled with culinary artwork. The menu is rooted in Gallic classics, such as steak frites and onion soup. Comme Ça's no-reservation raw bar is a good place to pop in for some oysters and a glass of fizz, or order from the cheese counter and grab a spot in the back room.
8479 Melrose Avenue, T 323 782 1104, commecarestaurant.com

Murano

As one might expect from the name, you will be dining under striking handblown Murano chandeliers at this WeHo dazzler. Thanks to co-owner and DJ Sandy Sachs, the sound system is designed as part of the architecture, with subwoofers hidden in the furniture, so as the jazz and lounge sounds build into Euro disco and house, you can still hold a conversation. The bar/lounge, with its high-backed white-leather banquettes and chartreuse-coloured wall sconces, is the place to sip a Ketel One-based Cubano Murano with fresh lime accompanied by some Italian nibbles. *9010 Melrose Avenue, T 310 246 9118, murano9010.com*

Citrus at Social

Mark Zeff's design, awash with lime green, orange and lemon yellow, is like diving into a fruit bowl. It's a fittingly vibrant backdrop for celebrated chef Michel Richard's menu of 'Lobster Begula Pearls' served in a tin, couscous coloured with squid ink, and his take on a Kit Kat bar with sauce noisette.
6525 Sunset Boulevard, T 323 337 9797, citrusatsocial.com

The Penthouse at The Huntley Hotel

Once part of a dowdy chain, The Huntley has been reborn as one of the top luxury hotels in the world. Design flourishes include a lobby with African fertility chairs, wooden drum tables and a check-in counter topped with inlaid stingray skin. But the real draw here is The Penthouse bar, which has an ethereal atmosphere thanks to its white-draped windows and views that stretch from Malibu to Palos Verdes. One of the best places in LA to watch the sun go down, this is where the west-side élite start their evening. Join them at the oval bar, where the tipple of choice is a mojito.
1111 Second Street, T 310 394 5454,
thehuntleyhotel.com

Dresden Restaurant

Yes, the Dresden, in fashionable Los Feliz,
is that bar from the film *Swingers*. And
everyone knows it's that bar that featured
in *Swingers*. But, hey, it's that bar from
Swingers just like you thought it would be:
cool. Lounge act Marty and Elayne haven't
let film fame or celebrity fans (Tom Petty
featured them in one of his music videos)
go to their heads. They celebrated 25
irony-free years of playing at the Dresden
in 2006 and plan to go on for many
years yet. The crowd is decidedly more
arch than the music, but the bartenders'
Cosmopolitans are the real thing,
and the white-leather décor makes for
an authentic Golden Age ambience.
*1760 N Vermont Avenue, T 323 665 4294,
thedresden.com*

CUT

Located in the Beverly Wilshire, best known as the *Pretty Woman* hotel, is the highly anticipated Wolfgang Puck steakhouse CUT and the Sidebar lounge, both by renowned architect Richard Meier, also responsible for The Getty Center (see p068). The two spaces are connected through the lobby by a linear canopy that lets light sparkle down on Eames-style black-mesh aluminum chairs and oak tables, all custom-designed by Meier. Puck's melt-in-your-mouth Japanese Wagyu beef and Kobe ribs cooked for eight hours with Indian spices definitely seem to have won over the A-listers. *Beverly Wilshire, 9500 Wilshire Boulevard, T 310 275 5200, fourseasons.com/ beverlywilshire*

Republic Restaurant + Lounge

Restaurant row has another star with Republic. Owner Mikayel Israyelyan enlisted designer Margaret O'Brien to set the stage – guests enter through the bar, past large leather sofas, a python-upholstered bar, granite tops and glass-beaded wall finishes. The dining room houses a 6m-tall wine tower, deer-antler chandeliers and a huge cylinder fire pit shaded by stainless-steel chain mail. The patio features sleek cabanas and giant parchment paper light fixtures by artist William Leslie. Executive chef Karim D Mejia serves up a contemporary American menu with a slightly Southern flair. His prime *filet* is thick as a brick – order it with a side of truffle grits.
650 N La Cienega Boulevard,
T 310 360 7070, therepublicla.com

STK

Successfully imported from New York's Meatpacking district is this high-energy 'female friendly' steakhouse with a conscience and plenty of sex appeal. Owned by The One Group, which also brought the LA nightlife scene One Sunset (T 310 657 0111), ICRAVE Design Studio has used the signature cream, black and purple for many of the rooms at STK. The fickle nightlife crowd has plenty of areas to enjoy a meal or attract attention, from the main dining room, bistro room, outdoor atrium, clubby Coco de Ville with a DJ or the adjacent verandah. Executive chef Todd Miller brings his signature shrimp 'rice krispies' and foie gras French toast, along with decadent steaks topped with black truffles or foie gras butter. *755 N La Cienega Boulevard, T 310 659 3535, theonerestaurants.com*

Katsuya

Master sushi chef Katsuya Uechi and Philippe Starck's latest creation offers diners both a visual and culinary feast. The ceiling features images of kimonos and *geta* (traditional geisha sandals), the walls are adorned with giant, blown-up photos of pouting lips and fluttering eyes, while sushi knives suspended in blocks of resin add a masculine edge. Expect a youthful Hollywood and Vine crowd

sipping on sake cocktails or Katsuya's signature Burning Mandarin (chilli-infused vodka mixed with lemon, orange and a dash of cranberry juice), while nibbling on albacore tuna with crispy onion and yellow tail sashimi with sliced jalapeños.
6300 Hollywood Boulevard,
T 323 871 8777, sbe.com/katsuya

Beso
Meaning 'kiss' in Spanish, chef Todd
English's and *Desperate Housewives* star
Eva Longoria Parker's upscale Latino
eaterie is pure glam, from the metallic
faux-crocodile-skin booths to the
delicately dripping crystal chandeliers.
Designer Tracie Butler has offset it with
an open kitchen and a ceviche bar on ice.
6350 Hollywood Boulevard,
T 323 467 7991

Foxtail
The supperclub is back, and this one is already being hailed as a 'modern-day Brown Derby', set up as it was by a handful of Hollywood power players, including SBE CEO Sam Nazarian and nightclub promoter Brent Bolthouse. Franklin Studios' palette features emerald green, silvery pink and touches of brass to create a very sexy, opulent environment; at ground level, art deco and nouveau influences mingle with 1970s London rock'n'roll chic. After gin cocktails and sampling chef Antonia Lofaso's innovative European bistro fare, such as tuna tartare and pappardelle with lamb ragout, head upstairs to the dance club, where DJs spin late into the night as the crowd spills out onto the patio.
9077 Santa Monica Boulevard,
T 310 859 8369, sbe.com/foxtail

Osteria Mozza

With a vibe leaning towards New York tavern rather than trattoria, Osteria Mozza prides itself on Italian food like you'd find in the mother country – think pig's trotter fried like a croquette and warm *trippa alla parmigiana*. It's all served in grown-up surroundings featuring mint green walls, high ceilings, low-slung lighting fixtures, brown leather banquettes and darkwood accents. Celebrity-chef owners Mario Batali and Nancy Silverton and restaurateur Joseph Bastianich also run the boisterous Pizzeria Mozza (T 323 297 0101) next door. Head here for paper-thin-crust pizza with bubbling cheese and unique toppings such as fennel sausage, rounded off with a glass of wine from their own Bastianich-Batali label.
6602 Melrose Avenue, T 323 297 0100, mozza-la.com

The Edison

When locals crave a fix of the once-forbidden 'green fairy', they head to this former power station, where the absinthe fountain flows freely. Transformed into a multi-lounge space by Andrew Meieran and Marc Smith, who has just completed Santa Monica's Shangri-La Hotel (T 310 394 2791), the bar has an underground speakeasy feel, with concrete walls splashed with murals by a local artist.

Order a Hemingway with champagne and absinthe – otherwise known as 'death in the afternoon' – and sink into a leather armchair in the Generator Lounge or Boiler Room. On Thursday nights patrons clamour for the 35-cent martinis, and at those 1910 prices, everyone drinks like it's the dawn of prohibition.
108 W Second Street, T 213 613 0000, edisondowntown.com

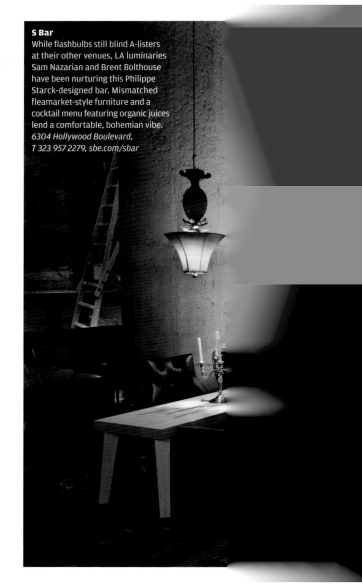

S Bar
While flashbulbs still blind A-listers
at their other venues, LA luminaries
Sam Nazarian and Brent Bolthouse
have been nurturing this Philippe
Starck-designed bar. Mismatched
fleamarket-style furniture and a
cocktail menu featuring organic juices
lend a comfortable, bohemian vibe.
6304 Hollywood Boulevard,
T 323 957 2279, sbe.com/sbar

INSIDER'S GUIDE

JODIE DOLAN, FASHION DESIGNER

Designer Jodie Dolan is a rising star on the fashion scene. Her clothing collections lean towards London-meets-West Coast cool and she has gained a loyal following in fickle LA.

Living in newly hip Beverly Hills, Dolan likes to take a stroll on Bedford Drive to the newsstand to pick up a style bible such as *10 Magazine*. For a bite to eat, you'll find her at the tiny Californian/French restaurant Hatfield's (7458 Beverly Boulevard, T 323 935 2977) with an order of scallops. A little more avant-garde is Wilson (8631 Washington Boulevard, T 310 287 2093), with its cool vibe and patio. Dolan likes to head to Angelini Osteria (7313 Beverly Boulevard, T 323 297 0070) for the Italian cuisine and friendly waiters, or Madeo (8897 Beverly Boulevard, T 310 859 0242) for great people-watching and old-school food. A snack of tacos and beer at El Carmen (8138 W Third Street, T 323 852 1552) is another treat, while she says that the martinis at Sidebar (Beverly Wilshire hotel, 9500 Wilshire Boulevard, T 310 275 5200) can't be beaten.

Shopping and inspiration can be found on villagey Melrose Place, at Temperley (8452 Melrose Place, T 323 782 8000) and Marc Jacobs (8400 Melrose Place, T 323 653 5100). To chill out Dolan heads to Power Yoga (1410 Second Street, T 310 458 9510) or Bikram Yoga (1862 La Cienega Boulevard, T 310 838 8040), or she goes for a drive with friends up the coast to Santa Barbara. *For full addresses, see Resources.*

ARCHITOUR
A GUIDE TO LA'S ICONIC BUILDINGS

As befits the city of the second chance, the built environment of Los Angeles has been constantly reinvented and reformulated, with a dizzying disregard for the past. Only a few poor adobe buildings date from the city's foundation, and then there's the Bradbury Building (304 S Broadway), one of the few 19th-century structures still standing. It was only after WWI that the city began to expand and established its indiscriminately exotic (okay, chaotic) look. Everything from reinterpreted haciendas to Beaux Arts Egyptian tombs were put up. This was the period of Grauman's Chinese Theatre (6925 Hollywood Boulevard, T 323 464 8111) and the pyramid-topped art deco City Hall (200 N Spring Street).

No architour of LA could do the city justice without taking in the midcentury domestic buildings designed by Frank Lloyd Wright and his disciples, Richard Neutra, Rudolf M Schindler and John Lautner. Highlights include Wright's Hollyhock House (see p070) and Ennis House (2655 Glendower Avenue, ennishouse.org), used as a set for *Blade Runner,* Schindler's Lovell Beach House (1242 W Ocean Front, Newport Beach), and Neutra's Lovell Health House (4616 Dundee Drive). In 1949, Lautner's wood-and-glass design for a coffee shop called Googie's on Sunset Strip spawned a new, futuristic style of architecture. Many Googie gems still exist, one of the most characterful being Norms Restaurant (see p012). *For full addresses, see Resources.*

Case Study House No 8

This landmark 1949 house-cum-studio, set on a bluff in the Pacific Palisades, is an icon of midcentury modern architecture. The property, designed by Charles and Ray Eames, was originally intended as part of the Case Study House Program for John Entenza's *Arts & Architecture* magazine, but so attracted the couple as the ideal live/work space that they decided to make it their home. An open courtyard separates the living and working quarters, which are filled with the furniture, objects and art installed by the owners. The glass-clad exterior is punctuated by primary-coloured panels. Visits to the house must be arranged at least 48 hours in advance.
203 Chautauqua Boulevard,
T 310 459 9663, eamesfoundation.org

Chemosphere
Julius Shulman's iconic photographs
might have made this John Lautner
building a bit too familiar for some, but
there's no substitute for seeing first hand
what an architect of genius could do with
a tiny budget of £17,000, in a vertiginous
mountainside location. The 45-degree
slope imposed serious constraints, but
apparently none at all to the architect's
imagination. For years, it had a 'For Sale'
sign up and was parodied on *The Simpsons*
as the mad, modern monstrosity that
no one would buy, though it was eventually
sold. Architect Frank Escher was hired by
the new owner to restore the Chemosphere
to something approaching its original state
– a revamp that earned the property an
award from the Los Angeles Conservancy.
Today, Lautner's classic stands as a
symbol of 1960s optimism and of today's
midcentury real-estate mania.
776 Torreyson Drive, johnlautner.org

Getty Center

Perched 273m above sea level in the foothills of the Santa Monica Mountains, Richard Meier's Bauhaus-influenced, international-modernist building literally dazzles. With its 40,000 white-enamelled panels, travertine stone cladding and, most importantly, the bright LA light that flows in through its open-plan entrance and plazas, this is a museum for the kind of Angelenos who don't like to take off their sunglasses. The art galleries are illuminated by windows and skylights with computer-controlled louvres and a system of artificial lights programmed to respond to the season and time of day in order to maintain optimum natural light. The view from the southern end, over the LA basin, is one of the best in the city.
1200 Getty Center Drive, T 310 440 7300, getty.edu

070

Hollyhock House

Sitting on top of a hill in Barnsdall Park, Hollyhock House was Frank Lloyd Wright's first LA-based project, taking advantage of what he coined 'California Romanza' – the freedom to make one's own form. Built between 1919 and 1921, Wright created a stunning house and garden while developing a regional style of SoCal architecture. Making full use of the local climate, the living space extends outdoors with porches, a courtyard and terraces with Hollywood Hills views. Named after the favourite flower of its owner, oil heiress Aline Barnsdall, the house is appropriately dotted with hollyhock motifs. In 1927, Barnsdall gave the house to the City of Los Angeles and today it functions as part of an arts complex as originally intended. *4800 Hollywood Boulevard, T 323 644 6269, hollyhockhouse.net*

SHOPPING

THE BEST RETAIL THERAPY AND WHAT TO BUY

As with most things in LA, the problem with shopping here is the excess of choice. The highest density of clothes and homewares shops lies in a square of West Hollywood that runs from Robertson Boulevard in the east to La Brea Avenue in the west, and principally along Beverly Boulevard, Melrose Avenue and Melrose Place. This is where you'll come across the ornate Hollywood Regency Phyllis Morris showroom, and her daughter's store, 655 Home (both at 655 N Robertson Boulevard, T 310 289 6868), Blackman Cruz (836 N Highland Avenue, T 323 466 8600) and Jonathan Adler (8125 Melrose Avenue, T 323 658 8390). If you're in the design trade, some of the showrooms in Cesar Pelli's Pacific Design Center (8687 Melrose Avenue, T 310 657 0800) may sell to you.

Moving east, Vermont Avenue, on the Los Feliz/Silver Lake borders, is packed with shops, including Show (1722 N Vermont Avenue, T 323 644 1960) for edgy designs, and Soap Plant/Wacko/ La Luz de Jesus (4633 Hollywood Boulevard, T 323 663 0122) for kitsch collectables. Another enclave is Silver Lake Boulevard, near Effie Street, where you'll find cool kitchen gadgets at Yolk (1626 Silver Lake Boulevard, T 323 660 4315). Venice offers the delightful store Surfing Cowboys (1624 Abbot Kinney Boulevard, T 310 450 4891), selling a magical mix of vintage furniture and ephemera, and the art gallery Obsolete (222 Main Street, T 310 399 0024). *For full addresses, see Resources.*

Mogul

Owner/designers Thomas Piscitello and Neal Wagner pay homage to the glitzy side of Tinseltown with furniture such as the 'Rossmore' bed, 'Trousdale' lounge chair and 'Lucite' cocktail table featuring materials like micro suede, white alligator skin, acrylic and chrome. Some of the fabrics come studded with Swarovski crystals, while signature accessories include skulls in handblown black glass and a pink 'Revolver' gun, and make lovely coffee table accent pieces. Standing in the middle of Melrose Avenue's design mecca, Mogul delivers high-fashion excess for those who aren't afraid to flaunt it. The store also offers paintings, 720-thread-count linens, bespoke creations, consultations and studio rentals.
8262 Melrose Avenue, T 323 658 5130, mogullife.com

Equator Books
An Abbot Kinney anchor tenant, this gallery and bookstore specialises in out-of-print art and photography books, and topics such as street culture, call girls and LA lore. Its interior, designed by Iraqi-born Rania Alomar, features layers of multi-ply intended to evoke piles of paper and books.
1103 Abbot Kinney Boulevard,
T 310 399 5544, equatorbooks.com

Woodson & Rummerfield's

The pieces in Ron Woodson and Jaime Rummerfield's House of Design range from midcentury modern to ultra-chic minimalist and Hollywood glamour. Their Woods & Fields collection fuses high style from the 1930s and 1940s with 1970s funkiness, and includes everything from wallpaper, sofas and mirrors to place mats and napkins. Head here if you aren't afraid to mix black lace tablecloths with red candlesticks and Rosenthal china. The design pair also specialise in modernist makeovers, with past projects including the remodelling of a Richard Neutra house in the Hollywood Hills, and the revamp of a Donald Wexler design in Palm Springs. *724 N La Cienega Boulevard, T 310 659 3010, wandrdesign.com*

A+R

Former film editor Andy Griffith and writer Rose Apodaca are the force behind this tiny store in Venice, which offers a quirky selection of goods from domestic and international artists and designers. Check out the goat's-milk soaps shaped like babies' hands (£11) or the 'Shoplifter' bag (£14) to get a flavour of the store. Each item comes with a tag describing the work and its maker, with featured pieces including tableware by Ego of Denmark and cardboard animals by Keisuke Saka. A+R is also big on unusual accessories, such as cast-resin belt buckles by Shane (£100) and necklaces fashioned from industrial washers by local artist Christie Frields.
1121 Abbot Kinney Boulevard,
T 310 392 9128, aplusrstore.com

Fred Segal

A favourite with A-listers, this upscale bazaar is the place for boutique shopping. Find the latest in designer homeware, or pick up premium jeans by Ron Herman. Pop into Apothia and choose from 200 handcrafted scents made from recherché ingredients such as Bulgarian rose and Javan vetiver.
8100 Melrose Avenue, T 323 655 3734, fredsegal.com

Boule

An offshoot of the original store in N La
Cienega Boulevard (T 310 289 9977),
this elegant pâtisserie and chocolatier
draws the crowds with its large macaroons
made from organic olive oil, lavender,
vanilla and black truffles. Chocolates of
choice include the Beckham Curry with
Moroccan gianduja, the Fleur de Sel
Caramels from Brittany and the Sicilian
pistachio Dante. Eclairs and Venezuelan
chocolate ice cream are also firm
favourites here. If that's all too rich for
your taste, the Intelligentsia coffee or
exclusive teas from Palais des Thès in
Paris should hit the spot. Shopping
for a gift? Infused olive oils, bamboo
chopping boards, Peugeot salt mills,
Chinese clay teapots and silver cocktail
spoons are sure to fit the bill.
*413 N Bedford Drive, T 310 273 4488,
boulela.com*

TableArt

Walter S Lowry and Stephen M Flynn chucked in their dull corporate jobs to open a shop devoted to fine dining and designer entertaining. The table settings change regularly, of course, and they sell dinnerware, glassware, linens and also tableware from Meissen, Nymphenburg, KPM and Augarten, among others. Notables include their own line of two-tone lacquered salad bowls (£48), a pair of outré sterling-silver 'Leopard' candlesticks (£1,315) by Argentia, and Anthologie Quartett's 'Leave the Light On' porcelain cube (£65), which comes topped with a bronze matchstick. You will see a lot of TableArt lines in upscale magazines, as the place is a honey trap for designers and creative directors. *7977 Melrose Avenue, T 323 653 8278, tartontheweb.com*

Twentieth

Owner Stefan Lawrence's 930 sq m temple of 20th-century design goes way beyond the usual suspects, incorporating an exclusive selection of lesser-known talent, and an in-house line of contemporary lighting and furniture called Twentieth Modern. The combined showroom and exhibition space also hosts an innovative rota of events. Twentieth attracts many film and television set designers looking for hip props, such as Mattia Biagi's 'Tar Mickey Mouse' (£1,020), Tejo Remy's 'Rag Chair' (£2,780) and Jason Miller lighting fixtures shaped like stag horns (from £150).
8057 Beverly Boulevard,
T 323 904 1200, twentieth.net

Kitson

Just a stone's throw from The Ivy
restaurant (T 310 274 8303) on Robertson
Boulevard, every young starlet's shopping
dream is fulfilled at Kitson. This is where
Tinseltown types such as Paris, Britney
and even Victoria Beckham shop for
oversized sunglasses, skinny jeans, chunky
bangles, bejewelled sandals, sparkly
lipgloss and scented candles. Featuring
a variety of speciality stores with cubic
metal windows, stark white interiors and
shockingly lurid graphics, Kitson also pulls
in the boys, who come for funky T-shirts
by Love & Eight, the latest Puma sneakers
and zip wallets by Marc by Marc Jacobs.
Don't forget to pick up your autographed
copy of Tori Spelling's book on the way out.
115 N Robertson Boulevard,
T 310 859 2652, shopkitson.com

Boom Studio
The huge HD Buttercup (T 310 558
8900) interiors warehouse in Culver
City is home to a wide range of stores,
including Boom Studio, a perfectly
formed outlet for Craig Varterian's
modernist furniture, such as the 'Metro
End Table' (£140), 'Hive Cube' shelving
(pictured; £57 per cube) and accessories.
*3239 Helms Avenue, T 310 202 1697,
boomusa.com*

SPORTS AND SPAS

WORK OUT, CHILL OUT OR JUST WATCH

Woody Allen was making jokes about LA's fitness fanaticism in the 1970s, and it hasn't got any less devout. The choices are dizzying, and subject to rapidly changing trends: Bikram yoga has recently given way to boot camps (where the bourgeoisie pay to be treated like conscripts). See and be seen at gyms such as The Sports Club/LA (1835 Sepulveda Boulevard, T 310 473 1447) and Equinox (8590 W Sunset Boulevard, T 310 289 1900), or get your car washed while you exercise at 24 Hour Fitness (15301 Ventura Boulevard, T 818 728 6777). Head to Exhale (1422 Second Street T 310 899 6222) in Santa Monica for a massage after a workout overlooking the sea, and hit the Sonya Dakar Skin Clinic (9975 Santa Monica Boulevard, T 310 553 7344) in Beverly Hills for some space-age skin pampering. At The Doves Studio (Unit B, 2000 Main Street, T 310 399 7654), you can try out a convertible hair colour that switches from blonde to brunette depending on how you brush it.

With no NFL team, baseball and basketball are the sporting passions in this city. Overburdened with big egos, the LA Lakers are the basketball team every other fan loves to hate, and tickets to see them at Staples Center (1111 S Figueroa Street, T 213 742 7340) aren't cheap. Since 1962, the LA Dodgers have played baseball at Dodger Stadium (1000 Elysian Park Avenue, T 323 224 1507). After a few decades in the doldrums they've recently returned to form. *For full addresses, see Resources.*

Spa Luce

It's hard to imagine that the traffic-logged Hollywood & Highland Center houses a tranquil 595 sq m boutique spa tucked in the top of the Renaissance Hollywood Hotel. The naturalistic design by Kerry Joyce includes a light-dappled reception with desk carved from a 300-year-old walnut tree (above), and faux-fur rugs throughout the white-enveloped main spa area. Nail technician Miyu Sudo, known for her A-list clientele including Alicia Keys, Gwyneth Paltrow, Alicia Silverstone and Jada Pinkett Smith, is on hand to prep nails for any season. Mere mortals can indulge in the five-part Japan Ritual massage or Hammam Ritual, or take in the city views from the rooftop pool.
Renaissance Hollywood Hotel,
1755 Highland Avenue, T 323 491 1376,
spaluce.com

Sunset Marquis Pool
Head to this legendary Mediterranean
villa-style hotel for a cooling dip in one
of its two pools. After a swim, soak up
the sunshine or dine in a tented cabana,
while tended to by the poolside butlers.
Or grab a drink at Bar 1200, just off the
lobby, a favourite haunt of rock stars
using the hotel's recording studio.
North Alta Loma Road, T 310 657 1333,
sunsetmarquishotel.com

Argyle Salon & Spa

For ludicrously luxurious pampering, it
doesn't get much better than this. Housed
in one part of the Sunset Tower Hotel,
formerly The Argyle, this 613 sq m, two-
floor treatment centre offers side-by-side
massages for couples, iPod plug-ins,
plasma screens, space for bridal-shower
spa outings, a white-marble Turkish
hammam, scrubs, wraps and whatever-
parts-you-want-waxed waxing. Try hair
stylist Mauricio Ribeiro's regenerative
Brazilian Blowout (£200 for 90 minutes),
or treat yourself to treatments including
acupuncture, collagen rejuvenation,
laser hair reduction, vitamin B12 injections
(to boost memory) as well as more
traditional grooming. This is the kind of
über-decadence that will make you feel like
a genuine member of the Hollywood A-list.
*Sunset Tower Hotel, 8358 Sunset
Boulevard, T 310 623 9000, argylela.com*

Venice Beach Recreation Center
Despite the tie-dyed tat and tattoo-tastic
feeling to the Venice boardwalk, it would
be a shame for any fit folk to come to LA
and not visit the ocean-front sports area,
better known as Muscle Beach. Set up
in 1934 in neighbouring Santa Monica
as a government-funded training ground
for dancers, gymnasts, bodybuilders and
circus acts, Muscle Beach claims to be
where all modern gyms have their origin.
The site moved to Venice in the 1960s,
but continued to attract the body beautiful
and those who just want to watch. Today,
as well as the pumped-up displays of
physical prowess, the recreation zone
offers basketball, tennis, handball and
volleyball courts – if you feel like joining
in, you can book through the centre.
1800 Ocean Front Walk,
T 310 399 2775, laparks.org

ESCAPES

WHERE TO GO IF YOU WANT TO LEAVE TOWN

What with it being a sprawling mega-city and all, it's tempting to think that it takes long enough to cover LA county without going further afield, but the surrounding area has plenty to tempt you onto the freeways or commuter planes out of town. The most scenic route north is Highway 1, the Pacific Coast Highway, which will take you to Spanish-flavoured Santa Barbara, but if you have time, take a diversion to the idyllic town of Ojai (pronounced 'Oh-hi') at the foot of the Topa Topa Mountains. North of Santa Barbara, those having a mid-life crisis may want to take Highway 101 to Buellton, in the Santa Ynez Valley, and the surrounding vineyard district, to recreate their own *Sideways* fantasy trip.

Also to the north, a long drive to Mojave and then taking US 395 and Highway 190 will give you a breathtaking trip into the Death Valley National Park (nps.gov/deva). You can actually fly to Vegas, but it's more iconic to do it the *Swingers*/gonzo way, driving overnight through the desert – just watch out for the giant bats near Barstow. Going south, you get to blandly pleasant San Diego. Although there are a number of ritzy towns, including La Jolla (pronounced 'La Hoya'), along the route, the best way to get there is to take a 50-minute flight from LAX. From San Diego airport, hop over the border to Tijuana – for all the religious kitsch, nasty booze and cheap prescription drugs you might, or might not, want.
For full addresses, see Resources.

Parker Palm Springs

The first hotel by America's design darling Jonathan Adler was worth the wait. His maxim is 'minimalism is a bummer', so it came as little surprise that, when he was commissioned to transform the former Givenchy Resort and Spa in Palm Springs, once owned by 1970s talk-show host Merv Griffin, he decided on a 'happy luxe' design philosophy, focusing on comfort and colour, as in the Rear Lounge (overleaf).

Another public space features a suit of armour ruling over a mix of retro and contemporary furniture (above). Each of the 12 one-bedroom villas and 131 rooms is different, but, for a special treat, opt for the two-bedroom Gene Autry Residence, which Adler describes as 'super-luxe'.
4200 East Palm Canyon Drive,
Palm Springs, T 760 770 5000,
theparkerpalmsprings.com

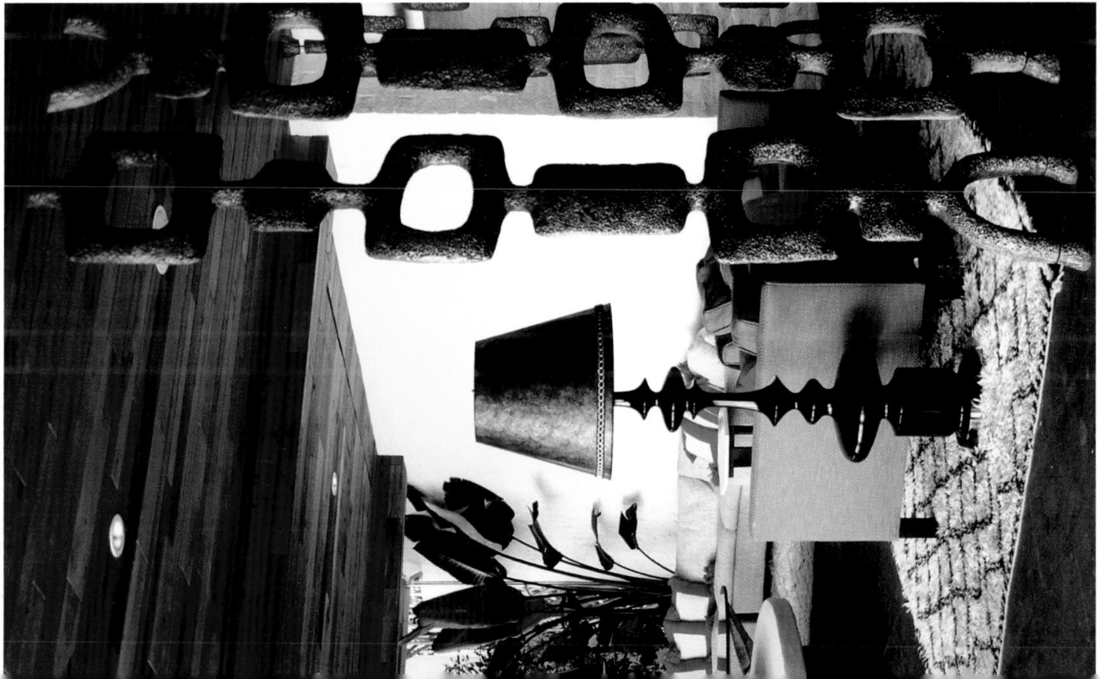

Post Ranch Inn, Big Sur
This hotel by the forest-trimmed coast
provides a soothing antidote to buzzy
LA. Stay in a new-age-meets-upscale
tree house, or a suite such as the Cliff
House (pictured), with glass and wood
walls, gun-metal fireplaces and concrete
floors. Chef Craig von Foerster has
a different tasting menu every night.
Highway 1, T 831 667 2200,
postranchinn.com

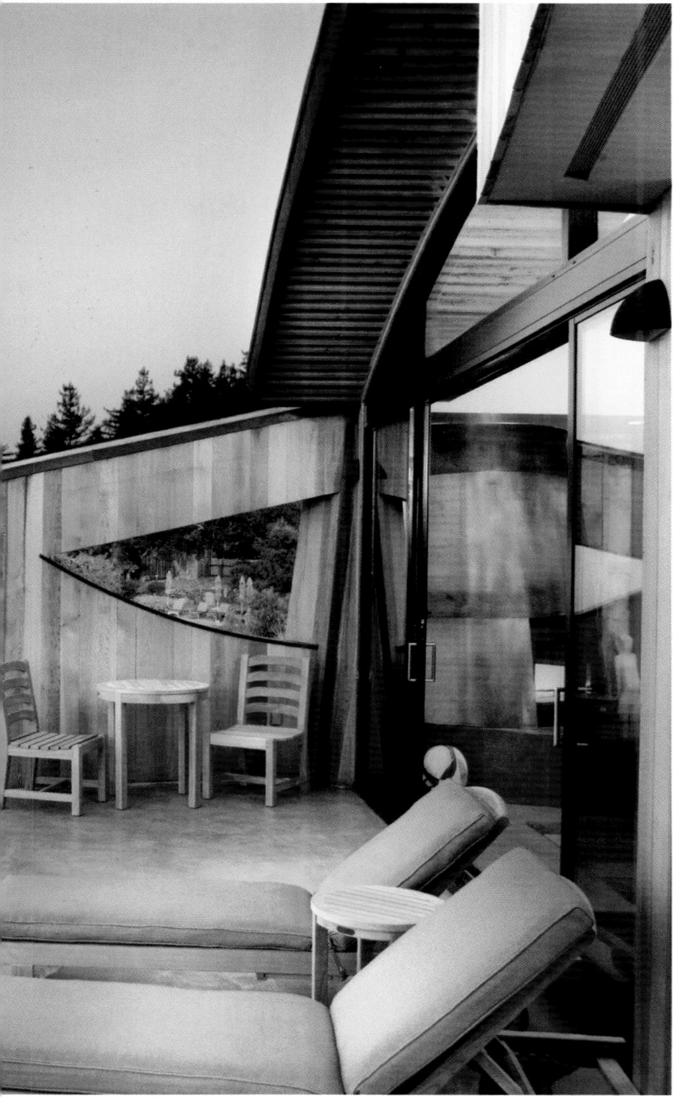

Cabo Azul Resort & Spa, Mexico

Being only a two-hour flight from LAX, SoCal residents like to think of Mexico's Los Cabos, or 'Cabo' as it's affectionately known, as their playground. So it made perfect sense to ship LA's most celebrated designer, Dodd Mitchell, in to create the Cabo Azul. The grounds are dotted with fire sculptures and whimsical waterscapes. The Penthouse Villas feel like a tented souk inside a genie's bottle with seductive lighting, exotic darkwood thatched canopy beds and metal lanterns. The view of the Sea of Cortez from the cool marble and mosaic chapel El Corazon (above) makes for a romantic wedding venue. Or unwind in the Mediterranean-themed PAZ Body & Mind spa with its crystal bath for two and outdoor treatment tables.
Los Cabos, T 877 216 2226,
caboazulresort.com

NOTES
SKETCHES AND MEMOS

RESOURCES

CITY GUIDE DIRECTORY

A

American Rag 032
150 S La Brea Avenue
T 323 935 3154
amrag.com

Angelini Osteria 062
7313 Beverly Boulevard
T 323 297 0070
angeliniosteria.com

Apothia 078
Fred Segal
8100 Melrose Avenue
T 323 651 0239
apothia.com

A+R 077
1121 Abbot Kinney Boulevard
T 310 392 9128
aplusrstore.com

Argyle Salon & Spa 092
Sunset Tower Hotel
8358 Sunset Boulevard
T 310 623 9000
argylela.com

B

Beso 054
6350 Hollywood Boulevard
T 323 467 7991

Bikram Yoga 062
1862 La Cienega Boulevard
T 310 838 8040
bikramyoga.com

Blackman Cruz 072
836 N Highland Avenue
T 323 466 8600
blackmancruz.com

BLD 033
7450 Beverly Boulevard
T 323 930 9744
bldrestaurant.com

Blue Velvet 032
750 S Garland Avenue
T 213 239 0061
bluevelvetrestaurant.com

BOA Steakhouse 041
The Grafton Hotel
8462 W Sunset Boulevard
T 323 650 8383
boasteak.com

BondSt 017
Thompson Beverly Hills
9360 Wilshire Boulevard
T 310 601 2255
bondstrestaurant.com

Boom Studio 086
3239 Helms Avenue
T 310 202 1697
boomusa.com

Boule 080
413 N Bedford Drive
T 310 273 4488
420 N La Cienega Boulevard
T 310 289 9977
boulela.com

Bradbury Building 064
304 S Broadway

C

Caltrans District 7 Headquarters 010
100 S Main Street

Capitol Records Building 013
1750 Vine Street
T 323 462 6252
capitolrecords.com

El Carmen 062
8138 W Third Street
T 323 852 1552

HOTELS
ADDRESSES AND ROOM RATES

Avalon 028
Room rates:
double, from $290
9400 W Olympic Boulevard
T 310 277 5221
avalonbeverlyhills.com

The Beverly Hills Hotel 032
Room rates:
double, from $515
9641 Sunset Boulevard
T 310 276 2251
thebeverlyhillshotel.com

Cabo Azul Resort and Spa 102
Room rates:
One-Bedroom Villa, from $350;
Penthouse Villa, from $750
Los Cabos
Mexico
T 877 216 2226
caboazulresort.com

Chateau Marmont 020
Room rates:
double, from $370
8221 Sunset Boulevard
T 323 656 1010
chateaumarmont.com

Hollywood Roosevelt Hotel 029
Room rates:
double, $400;
Cabana Suite, $1,200
7000 Hollywood Boulevard
T 323 466 7000
hollywoodroosevelt.com

The Huntley Hotel 046
Room rates:
double, $470
1111 Second Street
T 310 394 5454
thehuntleyhotel.com

The London West Hollywood 026
Room rates:
double, $350;
Suite 811, from $550
1020 N San Vicente Boulevard
T 310 854 1111
thelondonwesthollywood.com

Maison 140 016
Room rates:
double, from $220
140 S Lasky Drive
T 310 281 4000
maison140beverlyhills.com

Mondrian 016
Room rates:
double, from $400
8440 Sunset Boulevard
T 323 650 8999
mondrianhotel.com

Palihouse 018
Room rates:
double, from $300;
Room 311, from $750;
Holloway Loft Residence, from $2,000
8465 Holloway Drive
T 323 656 4100
palihouse.com

Hotel Palomar
Los Angeles-Westwood 022
Room rates:
double, from $350;
King Standard, from $350;
Vista King Spa Suite, from $460
10740 Wilshire Boulevard
T 310 475 8711
hotelpalomar-lawestwood.com

Parker Palm Springs 097
Room rates:
double, from $450;
One-bedroom villa, from $1,500;
Gene Autry Residence, $2,840
4200 East Palm Canyon Drive
Palm Springs
T 760 770 5000
theparkerpalmsprings.com

Post Ranch Inn 100
Room rates:
double, from $610;
Cliff House, from $2,415
Highway 1
Big Sur
T 831 667 2200
postranchinn.com

Raffles L'Ermitage 040
Room rates:
double, $885
9291 Burton Way
T 310 278 3344
beverlyhills.raffles.com

Hotel Shangri-La 016
Room rates:
prices on request
1301 Ocean Avenue
T 310 394 2791
shangrila-hotel.com

SLS 016
Room rates:
double, $400
465 N La Cienega Boulevard
T 310 247 0400
slshotels.com

The Standard Downtown 024
Room rates:
double, from $245;
Huge Room, from $325
550 S Flower Street/Sixth Street
T 213 892 8080
standardhotels.com

The Standard Hollywood 016
Room rates:
double, $215
8300 Sunset Boulevard
T 323 650 9090
standardhotels.com

Thompson Beverly Hills 017
Room rates:
King Superior, $495;
double, $605;
Penthouse Suite, $4,000
9360 Wilshire Boulevard
T 310 273 1400
thompsonbeverlyhills.com

Viceroy 030
Room rates:
double, $350
1819 Ocean Avenue
T 310 260 7500
viceroysantamonica.com

WALLPAPER* CITY GUIDES

Editorial Director
Richard Cook

Art Director
Loran Stosskopf
Editor
Rachael Moloney
Authors
Carole Dixon
Paul McCann
Deputy Editor
Jeremy Case
Managing Editor
Jessica Diamond

Chief Designer
Daniel Shrimpton
Designer
Lara Collins
Map Illustrator
Russell Bell

Photography Editor
Sophie Corben
Photography Assistant
Robin Key

Sub-Editor
Melanie Parr
Editorial Assistant
Ella Marshall

Interns
Karen Smith
Francesca Wilson

**Wallpaper* Group
Editor-in-Chief**
Tony Chambers
Publishing Director
Gord Ray

Contributors
Sara Henrichs
Meirion Pritchard
Ellie Stathaki

Wallpaper* ® is a
registered trademark
of IPC Media Limited

All prices are correct at
time of going to press,
but are subject to change.

Printed in China

PHAIDON

Phaidon Press Limited
Regent's Wharf
All Saints Street
London N1 9PA

Phaidon Press Inc
180 Varick Street
New York, NY 10014

Phaidon® is a registered
trademark of Phaidon
Press Limited

www.phaidon.com

First published 2006
Second edition (revised
and updated) 2009
© 2006 and 2009
IPC Media Limited

ISBN 978 0 7148 4904 1

A CIP Catalogue record for
this book is available from
the British Library.

PHOTOGRAPHERS

Rodolfo Arpia/Alamy
Capitol Records
Building, p013

Roger Davis
Caltrans District 7
Headquarters, pp010-011
Norms Restaurant, p012
Dresden, p048
Equator Books, pp074-075
TableArt, p082
Twentieth, p083

**Charles Ehlers/Rex
Features**
Los Angeles city view,
inside front cover

Tom Fowlks
STK, p051
Beso, pp054-055
Foxtail, pp056-057

Denis Freppel
Chemosphere, pp066-067

Giantstep Inc/Getty
Venice Beach Recreation
Center, pp094-095

Mark Harris
Katsuya, pp052-053
S Bar, pp060-061

Michael David Rose
The London West
Hollywood, p026, p027
BLD, p033
Joan's on Third, p036
Patina, pp038-039
Luckyfish, p041
The Penthouse at The
Huntley Hotel, pp046-047
Osteria Mozza, p058
The Edison, p059
Mogul, p073
Fred Segal, pp078-079
Boule, pp080-081
Kitson, pp084-085
Sunset Marquis Pool,
pp090-091

**Richard Ross/J. Paul
Getty Trust**
The Getty Villa, p037

Jeremy Samuelson
Parker Palm Springs,
p097, pp098-099

Tim Street-Porter/Esto
Hollyhock House,
pp070-071
Case Study House
No 8, p065

Alex Vertikoff
Getty Center, pp068-069

Matt Wignall
Jodie Dolan, p063

Lara Wilson
Walt Disney Concert
Hall, pp014-015

Facundo de Zuviria
BCAM at LACMA, pp034-035

LOS ANGELES
A COLOUR-CODED GUIDE TO THE HOT 'HOODS

WEST HOLLYWOOD AND MIDTOWN
Home to the city's gay community, who flock to the designer shops around Melrose Place

SANTA MONICA, VENICE AND CULVER CITY
These three neighbouring areas are at different levels of development, but are all on the up

HOLLYWOOD
Avoid the tourist tat of the Boulevard and visit the slick bars and clubs on the side streets

LOS FELIZ, SILVER LAKE AND ECHO PARK
Cool, very cool. Find boutiques and cafés among Neutra, Schindler and Lautner houses

BEVERLY HILLS AND WESTWOOD
Characterless but still unmissable, thanks to its moviestar glamour and the Getty Center

DOWNTOWN
Not a nice place to linger, but it's not the no-go zone of old. MOCA is worth the trip alone

For a full description of each neighbourhood, see the Introduction.
Featured venues are colour-coded, according to the district in which they are located.